FIREFIGHTERS
to the RESCUE

by Meish Goldish

Consultant: Don Howard
Fire Chief
Summit Fire District
Flagstaff, Arizona

BEARPORT PUBLISHING

New York, New York

Credits

Cover and Title Page, © RubberBall/SuperStock and Patricia Marks/Shutterstock; TOC, © SVLuma/Shutterstock; 4, © Ted Fitzgerald/Boston Herald; 5L, © AP Photo/John Cetrino; 5R, © Ted Fitzgerald/Boston Herald; 6, © Blue Shadows/Alamy; 7, © Ted Fitzgerald/Boston Herald; 8L, © AP Photo/The Gallup Independent/Jeffery Jones; 8R, © AP Photo/The Daily Sentinel/ Andrew D. Brosig; 9, © AP Photo/The Nashua Telegraph/Bob Hammerstrom; 10, © Radius/SuperStock; 11, © Blue Shadows/ Alamy; 12T, © Design Pics/SuperStock; 12B, © David Pino/Dreamstime; 13T, © Douglas R. Clifford/ZUMA Press/Newscom; 13B, © Robert Gallagher/ZUMA Press/Newscom; 14L, © Raymond Gehman/Corbis; 14R, © J. Baylor Roberts/National Geographic/ Getty Images; 15, © Guy Kitchens/ZUMA Press/Newscom; 16, © Guy Kitchens/ZUMA Press/Newscom; 17, © Justin Sullivan/ Getty Images; 18L, © AFP/Getty Images/Newscom; 18R, © Jon T. Fritz/MCT/Newscom; 19, © Lightroom Photos/USCG/Redux; 20L, © Mark E. Gibson/Corbis; 20R, © AP Photo/The Herald Bulletin/John P. Cleary; 21, © Alex Wong/Getty Images; 22, © Brad Rickerby/Reuters/Landov; 23, © Shannon Stapleton/Reuters/Landov; 24L, © Vincent L. Long/redbrickstock.com/Alamy; 24R, © Alamy; 25L, © Mark Bolster/LA Times; 25TR, © Mark Bolster/LA Times; 25BR, © Gene Blevins/ZUMA Press/Newscom; 26, © Big Cheese Photo/SuperStock; 27, © Rubberball/Photolibrary; 28T, © IndexStock/SuperStock; 28BL, © AP Photo/John Cetrino; 28BR, © Paul Heinrich/Alamy; 28–29, © Dale A. Stork/Shutterstock; 29, © Design Pics/SuperStock; 29BR, © Corey Sipkin/NY Daily News Archive/Getty Images; 31, © Rob Wilson/Shutterstock; 32, © Dwight Smith/Shutterstock.

Publisher: Kenn Goin
Editorial Director: Adam Siegel
Creative Director: Spencer Brinker
Design: Debrah Kaiser
Photo Researcher: Picture Perfect Professionals, LLC

Library of Congress Cataloging-in-Publication Data

Goldish, Meish.
  Firefighters to the rescue / by Meish Goldish ; consultant, Don Howard.
    p. cm. — (The work of heroes : first responders in action)
  Includes bibliographical references and index.
  ISBN-13: 978-1-61772-284-4 (library binding)
  ISBN-10: 1-61772-284-7 (library binding)
  1. Fire fighters—Juvenile literature. 2. Rescue work—Juvenile literature. 3. Fire extinction—Juvenile literature. I. Title.
  HD8039.F5G65 2012
  363.37023—dc22
                     2011005274

For more information, write to Bearport Publishing Company, Inc., 45 West 21st Street, Suite 3B, New York, New York 10010. Printed in the United States of America in North Mankato, Minnesota.

070111
042711CGA

10 9 8 7 6 5 4 3 2 1

Fire! 4

A Close Call 6

Job Training 8

Go, Team! 10

At the Station 12

Forest in Flames 14

Starving the Blaze 16

Disaster at Sea 18

Suited for Danger 20

Hundreds of Heroes 22

Rescue Me! 24

Why Be a Firefighter? 26

Firefighters' Gear 28

Glossary 30

Bibliography 31

Read More 31

Learn More Online 31

Index 32

About the Author 32

Fire!

In November 2007, a fire broke out in a three-story apartment building in Boston, Massachusetts. Flames quickly spread from the ground floor all the way up to the roof. Two children were trapped on the third floor. One of them, a six-year-old girl, was hanging out of a window to keep away from the deadly flames.

Firefighters used ladders to reach children trapped on the top floor.

A team of firefighters raced to the scene. While many of them fought to **extinguish** the blaze, one of them climbed a fire ladder to the third-floor window. He grabbed the **dangling** girl and brought her down to safety. The other child, however, was still trapped somewhere on the third floor. Would someone be able to find the young boy and get him out of the burning home in time?

In the United States, it usually takes firefighters about five minutes to reach the scene of a fire after receiving an alarm at the station.

Firefighters battled deadly flames and smoke in order to save people trapped in their apartment building.

A Close Call

As flames continued to destroy the building, firefighter Renard Miller entered the bedroom on the top floor. The thick black smoke from the fire made it almost impossible to see anything. Yet he heard the soft cries of a small child. Miller quickly felt his way around the edge of a bed in the smoky room. He found a two-year-old boy lying there. The firefighter tore off his face mask and put it over the boy's face to help him breathe.

face mask

air tank

To help with breathing, firefighters inside a burning building wear face masks that are connected to **air tanks**. They need this equipment because a fire produces smoke and poisonous gases in addition to burning up the **oxygen** people need to breathe.

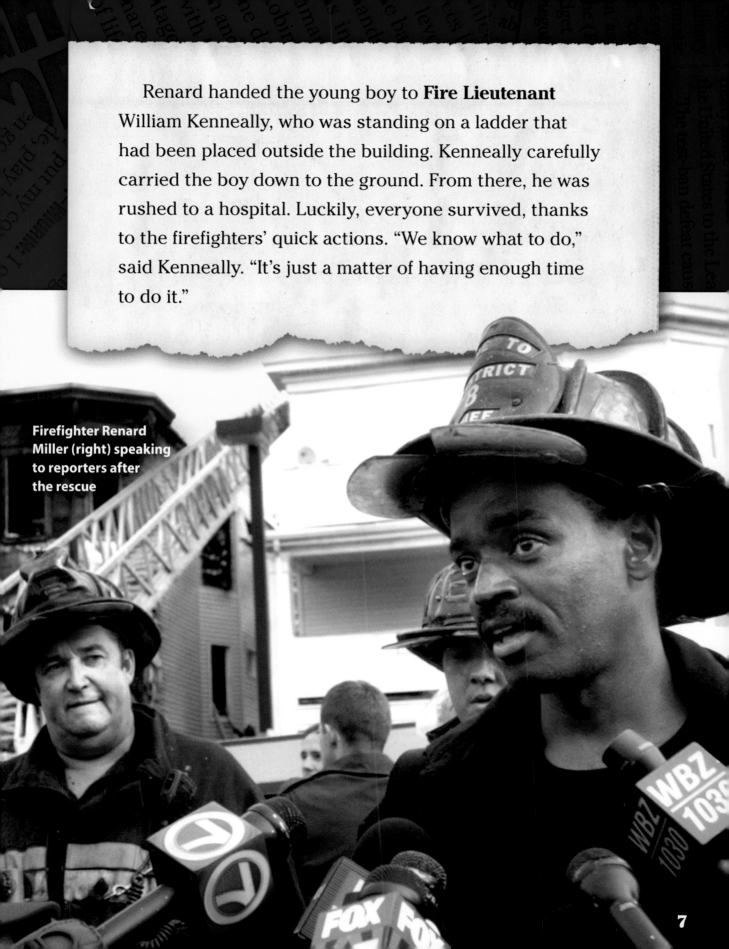

Renard handed the young boy to **Fire Lieutenant** William Kenneally, who was standing on a ladder that had been placed outside the building. Kenneally carefully carried the boy down to the ground. From there, he was rushed to a hospital. Luckily, everyone survived, thanks to the firefighters' quick actions. "We know what to do," said Kenneally. "It's just a matter of having enough time to do it."

Firefighter Renard Miller (right) speaking to reporters after the rescue

Job Training

Firefighters such as Renard Miller and William Kenneally must know exactly what to do to save lives in an emergency. To prepare for their job, they first go through a hard training period. They must pass tough **physical** tests, such as carrying 80-pound (36-kg) hoses and other heavy fire equipment. They practice rescues by carrying dummies that weigh as much as real people.

Firefighters use a dummy to practice lifting and moving a real fire victim.

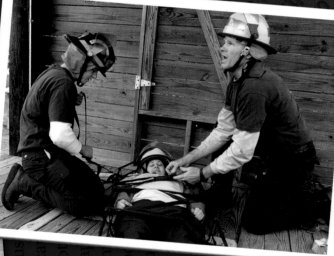

Trainees practice securely placing a person on a stretcher.

Most U.S. fire departments require firefighters to be at least high school graduates. Many also suggest that people who want to become firefighters take fire science classes at a college.

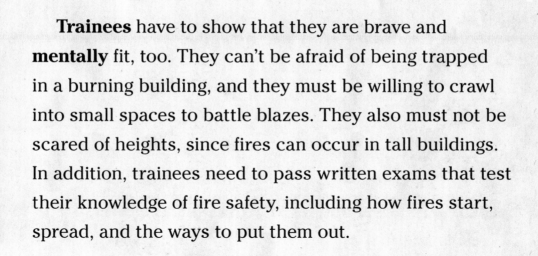

Trainees have to show that they are brave and **mentally** fit, too. They can't be afraid of being trapped in a burning building, and they must be willing to crawl into small spaces to battle blazes. They also must not be scared of heights, since fires can occur in tall buildings. In addition, trainees need to pass written exams that test their knowledge of fire safety, including how fires start, spread, and the ways to put them out.

Firefighters must be brave enough to battle flames at any height. This trainee is learning how to quickly climb down the outside of a building.

Go, Team!

During training, firefighters learn to work as a team. They are taught to never enter a burning building alone. Instead, a firefighter must stay with at least one other team member, or "buddy," at all times. Each buddy checks on the safety of his or her teammate during **exercises** and **drills**.

A firefighter always enters a burning building with at least one other team member.

On the job, firefighters continue to practice teamwork. They work in a group called a **company**, which is led by a **battalion** chief. At a fire, the chief assigns jobs to different firefighters, such as attaching hoses to **hydrants** or putting ladders in place. Company members cooperate with one another so their work goes quickly and smoothly.

Firefighting is a team effort. These firefighters practice attaching a hose to a fire hydrant.

Because a firefighter's assignment can change during a fire, each company member must know how to perform all types of firefighting duties.

At the Station

When they're not out rescuing people, firefighters are busy at their **fire station**. They check all the equipment that was used on the last job. They clean their masks and refill their air tanks. They examine the trucks, hoses, ladders, and tools to make sure they're in good working order for the next emergency.

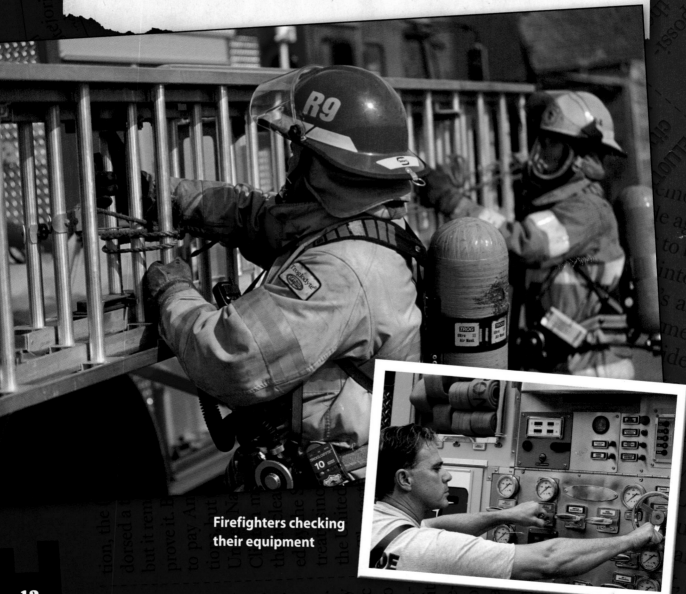

Firefighters checking their equipment

In many ways, the station is a home away from home for firefighters. Company members take turns cooking meals for the group. Since a work **shift** may last up to 24 hours, firefighters nap at the station as well. When the fire alarm sounds, they wake instantly—ready to hop onto the fire engine and rush out of the station.

Company members take turns shopping for food, preparing meals, and cleaning up.

Firefighters spend part of their time at the station practicing fire drills as well exercising to stay in shape.

Forest in Flames

Not all fires can be easily and quickly reached by fire trucks. For example, a fire may begin in a distant forest, where there are few, if any, roads. As a result, the flames can spread for several miles before fire trucks are able to arrive on the scene. So how do firefighters quickly get close enough to battle these blazes? They come down from the sky!

After firefighters parachute into the area near a forest fire, their tools, along with food and water, are dropped to them—also by parachute.

The first **responders** to a forest fire are **smoke jumpers**. These firefighters parachute down from airplanes. They land near the edges of the blaze. Their job is to **contain** the fire so that it doesn't spread any farther. The jumpers are followed by **hotshots**—groups of firefighters who arrive by trucks or other vehicles to help battle the flames.

 Firefighters at a forest fire may stay for days, weeks, or even months until the fire is finally put out.

Hotshots are trained to work in faraway areas with little outside help.

Starving the Blaze

How do smoke jumpers and hotshots contain a forest fire? They dig a large path called a **firebreak** around the blaze. All branches, **brush**, and other burnable materials are cleared away from the path. As a result, the flames can't spread any farther when they reach the firebreak because there's nothing left to burn. The fire is "starved" and goes out.

Pulaski

Firefighters create a strip of empty ground around a forest fire.

Firefighters dig a firebreak with a tool called a **Pulaski**. It's a combination ax and **hoe** that is used to clear away anything from the ground that may burn.

Airplanes and helicopters are also used to fight forest fires. Sometimes they drop buckets of water on the blaze. In larger fires, planes dump a **fire-retardant** chemical called "sky jello." It smothers the flames, forcing them to go out.

Sky jello is dropped on a fire to put out the flames.

Disaster at Sea

Not all fires are fought on land. In April 2010, an explosion occurred on the Deepwater Horizon—a giant **oil rig** that was digging a **well** about 42 miles (68 km) off the coast of Louisiana in the Gulf of Mexico. The blast produced tall flames that spread along the rig's platform. Luckily, most of the 126 workers on board managed to escape quickly in lifeboats.

The Deepwater Horizon before the explosion

The rig's explosion cracked a pipe that was connected to the oil well, causing more than 200 million gallons (757 million liters) of oil to flow into the Gulf.

Firefighters arrived on **fireboats** to battle the blaze. They sprayed thousands of gallons of water onto the flames. However, the raging fire, fueled by oil, could not be extinguished. It burned out of control for a day and a half. It finally went out after the weakened rig collapsed and sank into the water.

A fireboat uses the water around it to spray on a fire. Pumps shoot the water through hoses.

 The U.S. **Coast Guard** used boats and helicopters to rescue the rig workers from the water. Sadly, 11 workers were never found after the blast.

19

Suited for Danger

Firefighters don't only rush to the scene of a fire. Sometimes they are called to help out with nonfire emergencies, such as acid spilled from a truck, gas leaking from a pipe, or the release of **radioactive** materials from a building. In these situations, a hazmat team reports to the scene. This group of firefighters is specially trained to deal with **hazardous** materials.

Specially designed suits help to protect hazmat workers.

This hazmat team is trying to stop dangerous acid from spreading.

The word *hazmat* is short for "<u>haz</u>ardous <u>mat</u>erials." Some hazmat teams are trained to respond to nuclear, chemical, and biological weapons.

Hazmat team members work quickly to identify the dangerous materials and keep them from spreading. Each team member wears a **protective** suit that covers every inch of his or her body. It prevents the firefighter from touching and breathing dangerous chemicals. Like regular firefighters, the hazmat team is ready to race to an emergency 24 hours a day, 7 days a week.

In 2006, this hazmat team investigated a liquid that was mysteriously left at the Lincoln Memorial in Washington, D.C.

Hundreds of Heroes

Although firefighters protect themselves on the job, their lives are always at risk. On September 11, 2001, responders rushed to the World Trade Center in New York City after **terrorists** flew planes into the twin towers. Flames and smoke poured from the upper floors of the two 110-story office buildings.

About 2,800 people lost their lives in the September 11 attack on the World Trade Center.

The first firefighters at the scene were from **Squad** 18. They raced up the stairs of the North Tower to rescue trapped and injured people. Hundreds of other firefighters poured into both buildings to do the same. Unfortunately, no one knew that the towers were about to collapse. In all, 343 brave firefighters lost their lives during their heroic attempt to rescue the people from the burning towers.

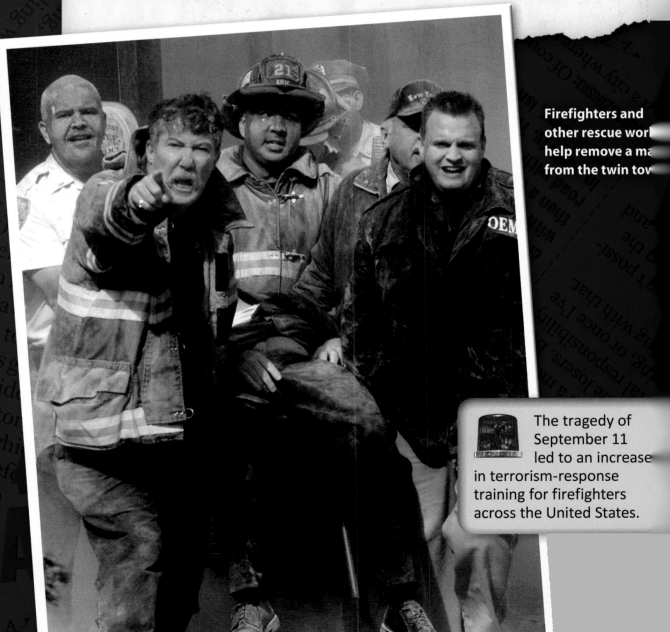

Firefighters and other rescue wor help remove a ma from the twin tov

The tragedy of September 11 led to an increase in terrorism-response training for firefighters across the United States.

Rescue Me!

Firefighters save many people trapped in fires. However, they often perform other kinds of rescues as well. They might be called to free a young boy who has accidentally locked himself in a room. They may also need to get people out of a car after an accident.

jaws of life

To rescue people trapped in a car, firefighters often use a tool called the "jaws of life." It works like a giant can opener to cut off the roof or doors of a badly damaged vehicle.

A firefighter uses the "jaws of life" to rescue a victim trapped in a car.

In January 2010, Joe St. Georges of the Los Angeles Fire Department saved a dog that had fallen into a fast-moving river. St. Georges was lowered by helicopter **cable** to the raging waters below so that he could scoop up the dog. Even though the frightened animal bit St. Georges on his thumb, the brave firefighter managed to hold on to the animal until they were both lifted to safety.

Joe St. Georges feared that if he didn't rescue the dog, an untrained person might try it and end up needing to be rescued as well.

Joe and the dog he rescued being lifted up to the helicopter

The dog was checked for injuries after the rescue.

Why Be a Firefighter?

Since firefighting is so dangerous, why would anyone take the job? Curtis Smith joined the Golden Valley Fire Department in Minnesota because he wished to help others in trouble.

"Sometimes bad things happen," said Smith. "I wanted to be part of the solution." He is always learning useful skills that make his job satisfying.

There are more than 1 million firefighters in the United States. About 46,000 are women.

Jenny Toavs is also a Golden Valley firefighter who enjoys the thrill of helping people. She also likes the strong friendships she's made with fellow workers. "You become like family," she said. "We help each other out in so many ways." Thanks to dedicated workers like these, people will always be able to rely on firefighters in an emergency.

Firefighters' Gear

Firefighters use different types of trucks to respond to different types of emergencies.

A *pumper truck* is the main truck in each fire company. Its controls allow firefighters to adjust the amount of water they pump onto a fire.

A *rescue truck* carries tools such as thick rope, poles, and the jaws of life, which may be needed to rescue someone who is trapped.

An *aerial truck* has a long ladder that is used to fight a fire in a tall building.

Firefighters use and wear special equipment on the job. Here is some of their gear.

The *helmet* is made of strong plastic that will not melt in a fire. Fireproof flaps protect the wearer's neck and ears.

The *turnout coat* is waterproof, fireproof, and protects the firefighter from acid.

The *face mask* lets the firefighter breathe easily by blocking out smoke.

An *ax* is used to break through walls and doors.

The *gloves* are fireproof.

The *air tank* holds about 15 to 30 minutes of air.

A *two-way radio* keeps firefighters in touch with one another while working.

Bunker pants protect a firefighter from getting burned on the legs.

The *boots* are so strong that it is difficult for nails to puncture them.

Glossary

air tanks (AIR TANKS) containers of oxygen that firefighters use so that they can breathe clean air

battalion (buh-TAL-yuhn) a large group organized to work together

brush (BRUHSH) a thick growth of small trees, bushes, and shrubs

cable (KAY-buhl) a thick wire or rope

coast guard (KOHST GARD) a branch of the military that protects a nation's coasts and comes to the aid of boats and ships in trouble

company (KUHM-puh-nee) a firefighting unit serving under the command of a battalion chief

contain (kuhn-TAYN) to keep under control

dangling (DANG-ling) swinging or hanging down loosely

drills (DRILZ) training activities that are practiced over and over

exercises (EK-sur-*syez*-iz) activities that are used for training

extinguish (ek-STING-gwish) to put out a fire or flame

fireboats (FIRE-bohts) boats used to fight fires in or near a body of water

firebreak (FIRE-brayk) a path cleared around a forest fire to stop flames from spreading

fire lieutenant (FIRE loo-TEN-uhnt) a person who directs some of the activities of a fire company

fire-retardant (*fire*-ri-TARD-uhnt) something that slows down the speed with which something burns

fire station (FIRE STAY-shuhn) a building where fire equipment is kept and where firefighters wait for their next emergency call

hazardous (HAZ-ur-duhss) dangerous

hoe (HOH) a gardening tool with a thick blade that is used to loosen earth and remove weeds

hotshots (HOT-shots) people who are trained to fight forest fires

hydrants (HYE-druhnts) large outdoor pipes connected to a water supply that is used in a fire emergency

mentally (MEN-tuhl-ee) having to do with the mind

oil rig (OIL RIG) an offshore platform used to drill for oil beneath the ocean floor

oxygen (OK-suh-juhn) a colorless gas that is found in the air and water, and that animals and people need to breathe

physical (FIZ-uh-kuhl) having to do with the body

protective (pruh-TEK-tiv) keeping something safe from harm

Pulaski (puh-LASS-kee) a firefighting tool that works as both an ax and a hoe

radioactive (ray-dee-oh-AK-tiv) giving off dangerous, invisible rays of energy

responders (ri-SPOND-urz) people who arrive at the scene of an emergency to provide help

shift (SHIFT) a set period of time in which a person works

smoke jumpers (SMOHK *juhmp*-urz) firefighters who parachute into a forest to battle a blaze

squad (SKWAHD) a small group of people who are trained to work together

terrorists (TER-ur-ists) individuals or groups that use violence and terror to get what they want

trainees (tray-NEEZ) people who are learning a new skill

well (WEL) a deep hole that people dig to get oil, water, gas, or steam

Bibliography

Downey, Tom. *The Last Men Out: Life on the Edge at Rescue 2 Firehouse*. New York: Henry Holt (2004).

Pickett, George. *The Brave: A Story of New York City's Firefighters*. New York: Brick Tower (2002).

Smith, Dennis. *Firefighters: Their Lives in Their Own Words*. New York: Broadway Books (2002).

Read More

Kalman, Bobbie. *Firefighters to the Rescue!* New York: Crabtree (2005).

Kelley, Alison Turnbull. *First to Arrive: Firefighters at Ground Zero*. Philadelphia: Chelsea House (2003).

Oleksy, Walter. *Choosing a Career as a Firefighter*. New York: Rosen (2000).

Thompson, Lisa. *Battling Blazes: Have You Got What It Takes to Be a Firefighter?* Minneapolis, MN: Compass Point (2008).

Learn More Online

To learn more about firefighters, visit
www.bearportpublishing.com/TheWorkofHeroes

Index

air tank 6, 12, 29

ax 16, 29

boots 29

Boston, Massachusetts 4

bunker pants 29

company 11, 13, 28

Deepwater Horizon 18–19

equipment 6, 8, 12, 29

face mask 6, 12, 29

fireboats 19

firebreak 16

fire station 12–13

fire trucks 12, 14, 28

forest fires 14–15, 16–17

gloves 29

Golden Valley Fire
   Department 26–27

hazmat team 20–21

helmet 29

hoses 8, 11, 12, 19

hotshots 15, 16

jaws of life 24, 28

Kenneally, William 7, 8

Los Angeles Fire Department
   25

Louisiana 18

Miller, Renard 6–7, 8

New York City 22

oil rig 18–19

Pulaski 16

sky jello 17

Smith, Curtis 26

smoke jumpers 15, 16

St. Georges, Joe 25

teamwork 10–11

Toavs, Jenny 27

training 8–9, 10, 15, 20, 23

turnout coat 29

two–way radio 29

U.S. Coast Guard 19

World Trade Center 22–23

About the Author

Meish Goldish has written more than 200 books for children. His books
Bug-a-licious and *Michael Phelps: Anything Is Possible!* were Children's Choices
Reading List Selections in 2010. He lives in Brooklyn, New York.